Book Three: Illusions of Existing

Candice Louisa Daquin

Printed in the United States of America

First Printing, 2016

ISBN 978-1-329-86210-4

TheFeatheredSleep Press ©

San Antonio, Texas

LIBRARY OF CONGRESS CATALOGUING IN PUBLICATION DATA

Daquin, Candice.

Illusions of Existing.

Poems.

ISBN 978-1-329-86210-4 (pbk.)

Poetry Collections by Candice Daquin

Book One: A jar for the jarring (2013)

Book Two: The bright day has gone child and you are in for the dark (2013)

Book Three: Illusions of existing (2014)

Book Four: Sit in fever (2014)

Book Five: We hide as much as we seek (2015)

Book Six: The war against becoming yourself (2015)

Book Seven: Pollination (2016)

The feathered steel

PRESS

Dedicated to Jack. You have the heart of the world within you.

Table of contents

My faithless

Artificial appetites

Auditioning patience

Haunted ambelic

Grief and the beautiful girl with tattoos

Illusions of existing

The Waxen Effigy and the Real Estate Agent

It's a socialist Jewish thing

Lie to me

At least we are all alien

Dead bird

The Father figure

Past tense, present absent

Compulsion's riddle

Twin

Mercurial

Your hands in mine

Rabbit Heart

The uterus is surgically absent

No memory of the ocean

Leaching life from the tallest

The reluctance of endurance

Tight symmetry

Eclipsed detach

All the time in the world

Girl of the sky

French for tongue

Turning orange

Mercurial, fucked in the head, or just thinking?

Without my interjection

That's like having a glass heart

What do I know?

Positioned in naught

Cocoon

Expected

Who leaves behind

Yellow circles

Coming up for air

Plastic swimming caps

The hour collapses willingly upon us

Hiroshima 70

Water

The Devil's Instant (or an ode to hating small talk)

The urge to ask for life after we are dead

Not even hemlock

Hurry

The short life

The war of welts

Absorbed paper cost

Burst eardrums

Old man's hunger

Return me time

Invert

Reflection's advice

Scorpion

Acts and intervals

Tabula-rasa

Running out of air

Granny the commie

Damselfly

Kiss Kiss

Infasound

The Firebird

Always believed vengeance had no place
Then coiling out, familiar in terrible way, seen in dream
A serpent of anger, viper of pay back
Flung from abyss into consciousness
All suddenly red with rage tightly shuttered
Was I really sitting on this box of snakes all these years?
Waiting without knowing, unleashing a storm of fury
Burning in my skin, red eyes, angry sky
All is molten and ragged, transformed in a blink
This is not me, and it is more than ever before, a truth

Resolve the puzzle claiming Sanity's return?
Yet I want to exist in this fury like a fire bird
Breathing all chained words with golden flame
In strange ways I am protected by suddenness, no time for rejection
From cold neurotic powerless howl
I'm scaling worlds with talons, tearing down lies with bird of prey fierceness
A firebird in body of stillness, cold water, bitten tongue, pigeon feet
I leave my former shape to slump and snore through battle, I explode into light and fly

If you say so

Her accent;
A snob, someone who thinks she's better than others
Who the HELL does she think she is?
Guilty! Guilty!

Her clothes;
Black in Summer?
Too ostentatious
She's not from here
What's she trying to prove?
Setting herself apart for attention
Isn't she too old for that?

Her weight;
On some funny diet
Only eats organic bananas
People like that make me sick
Picky eater, eating disorder
Skinny jeans, shrunken head

Her skin;
Does she ever go out in the sun?
Get a tan! Get some color!
Her legs glow in the dark!
I wouldn't wear that!

Her home;
Have you seen her shelves?
All she does is read!
She's never watched reality TV!
She thinks she's better than us
She has an attitude of superiority

Her silence;
She doesn't talk much?
She never wants to go eat with us all!
She isn't a joiner, a team player
She doesn't like bowling!
People from "over there" always feel superior

if you say so
Then it must be true
Right?

Night circles

If it had been me, or my turn. You would have been there, as once you tried. I would not have needed you then, it's how I cope, I rationalize my emotions into pockets and end up collecting marbles instead of people.

Your need, it runs as deep as tumors, it's part of your very fabric. In that love me/hate me see saw, you alternately repel and suffocate. I balance in middle, where you stretch to reach your mercurial Everest and wet Poseidon.

Long years, as much as I know how, I danced to find ways of satisfying you. It was never enough, just as words rarely are. In times of trauma it's not touch or caress that comforts me. My skin flinches contact like a fish gasping for the echoing solitude of ocean or deep pond. I always return there, it's how I evolved.

You turn to spotlight succor and strain closer to sun when beating fast, your heart constricts with fear. Advertising for attention and comfort like a seal whilst I slip wordless into the sea. Even a thousand hands holding you would not calm the hunger in your eyes for more.

Though oil and water cancel each other out, I hoped my existence filled your empty vases, but time like wrinkles, traverses truth, showing cruelty in unfiltered light, our errors and scattered best hope for romanticized foolery.

Perhaps in my interpretations I miss this basic truth, a shape of fate fashioned before we knew, eaten with every action and a spasming reflux of I Told You So. No surprise then, my absent heart, my empty arms, uninviting, keening toward escape.

In that cruelest of reduction, like a mirror I see my future, the dull thud of inevitable and inescapable. This, white in night wet chalk, draws conclusion and fate into lurching dance. It is true, wherever you go, there you are, and my child within blanches at unavoidable futures like a shrinking widow hugs the wall, turning with nightfall into a hundred pieces of a long held circle.

Without weight

In the night
That airless hour
Cool tile, thick air
Curtains heavy, clocks loud in quiet
Faraway hums and chirp
The unseen in dark
Her walk
Through dew laced grass
Colorless in moon
Where do the animals go?
Stars like escaping filament
Strangely sound and then silence
As if tigers, bears, large monsters
Climb and pick through flower and thick
A world rising and falling
As we sleep, or, without noise
Unlatch the gate for escape

When you go

When you go
Shall I remain?
In the soft eventide
Of love's dried and velvet shame

When you go
Shall I remain?
Slipping into silvered catkin
Roasted chestnuts sleeping in shivered skin

When you go
Shall I remain?
Behind feigning wisteria
Rosé licks wrapped in paisley weary

When you go
Shall I remain?
To empty space with love
In burnished ache and fatigued wane

Green fly in sun

Mustard, thick and lazy
Sits globular, swollen in tit
Green fly in sun
Warm against tile
Green like wet leaves in June
Like lizards wiggling against
Tall pampas grass
These
Purify
The
Day

Mosaic

The sharpest taste of aching feathers dyed dim by winking corridors
Forgetting room number, floor, wing, suite
So many names to describe boxes we fear dying in
TV's droning distractions, whir of fan
A chemical smell leaching into bleached space
Carry me out, public spectacle, a Jill in the Box, useless coil around human lifeline
Cupboards of tired deflates, where did the people go? Left with spinning tops
Survive outside wombs of hissing compressors, waxen floors, disinfected fetal viability
Chew it over, abort lunch, threaten paranoia, what's at the bottom of the pail? Inside
bandages? Behind frosted windows?
Where does bright life and contracted sterility merge and find reprieve in balmy step from
unhooked machines, bearing fangs in mosaic agreement?
Because it's fallen, because it's ragged and claimed by the wind, wrapping and curling
through confined space devoid of life

Disconnected number

You call
It's your voice
A low mumbling in my head
Self-generated thunder
Darkness covering my laughter
I laugh when it's horrific
When it's a nightmare
At funerals
I don't mean to
It boils out of me unbidden
Crazed, wanting explanation
For unexplainable
You call
I hear what you say
I hear myself answer
I am already far away

Failure of concern

All her life a voice told her she wasn't as caring as best intentions. It doesn't come naturally. What comes naturally is a longing for avoidance and running away. Caring is easy it's just a word. Following through is what separates wheat from chaff. She is the chaff. She smiles, looks concerned, her heart even aches, inside she stands behind, an empty heart longs to escape.

Was it the way she grew up? Is it being an only child? Did bullying close off her empathy, or the loss of another friend, diminish her faith in humanity? Maybe there was no faith to diminish? Could she have skated, the frozen girl, through life, thinking her vegetarian ways and love of animals and orphans, albinos and pigeons, even the diseased ones, would make her what she was not?

Going to church once, shaking as the others shake, for answers to gall into her myopic lap, she could separate those who said God Bless You automatically and promise with vacant eyes to pray for you, from those whose hearts gave all they had and then some. She didn't belong in either camp. She wouldn't leave you bleeding or cause it but with all the fiber of her being she would feel infected by your unwitting deterioration and then, ashamed and wrong for wanting to run as much as stay. You could be dying, you could be living, and her confusion in spirit would ring falser than those who rise in time of need, a flag, a wagon, the American Spirit, the Wounded Warrior, a mother, a father, a child.

She had no experience of being a parent but knew that was no guarantee of membership into the empathy club. What would unlock her sometime paused heart and set sentiment free, she couldn't say. When people milled around and prayed with you, exchanging stories to one another of former ills, whilst making blankets or checking cancer statistics, she roosted alone on the periphery where she fit in, as close to the ledge as possible.
Her gallantry is found in short lived gesture and well spun words, in our idea that we're all the same when that's never been true. Her heartlessness resides in not recognizing the shift from familiar loved one to sick waxen sufferer. It appalls her, shows her the deformation of her empty words, the corruption or lack of conscience and an unbearable truth.

Everyone can die. Leave a room and when gone, that room stops inhabiting their energies, slowly it grows cold and drab, until it is just a room. As surely as she can see the karmic surmount of her eventual fate, the lines from good to bad blurred and wanting, she sees too that none of us exist, and she does not exist, and the chorus, the face paint, the flowers, the empty room and finally, a window flung open to air, is how she is, misted by rain behind her fixed stare and tied to duty and betrayal both, by a human chord she neither recognizes nor needs. She is, as she realizes now, from somewhere else, and this, all of this, is a foreign language she has no answer for.

Wisdom's color

The senility of the sane
Begets wisdom

Sometimes
More
Is less

Sometimes
Broken
Is
Whole

When the last
Word
Is emptied
Of artifice

Birds
Green and violet
In silver reflection
Will
Watercolor
Skies

Universal
Relief
In
Undoing
Learned
Ways
That
Blind
Student

Truth
Alone
Flies
Ahead of
Word

In deed there rests
The sloping path

Swimming without breath

The shelved scream
Postponed indefinitely
Sat collecting revenge
In obscure recess

Invariably surfacing
In stifled fit and sudden silence
A red rage darkening edges
Staining sock, toe, avoidance

Too long, bandaged, muffled
Filed under mistaken strength
Suffocating for want, for release
In quiet funeral taboo

Asunder our vibrating hollows
Damming with thirsty attempt
Perpetual sickness coiling inward
Straining breeches of sense

This ill journey no more makes
Pain retreat, curtsey and bow
Though in amber we preserve
Its dying cries infecting truth
Like swimming without breath

A place eyes do not see

(How do you write down what has no words? Convey feelings without language to describe them?)

Trying with sense
Life sleeping in decent
Falling rustle
Faded cotton
Bedsheets of long and often
Warmth in rooms walked into
Whilst home remains frozen over

If
That
Charm around my neck
Made of green stones from river beds
Fabrication takes ten
Let them all in
All the metal teeth
Make them dinner, telling stories
Of wide lies and hissing space
Gaps of sense
Time displaced
So much, you, turning slow
So much to say, words
Crumbled by heat, unexplained
Dents in fabric

This isn't happening
Under water
Your call
Reconciled bird
Wounded wing glinting gold
Loose, fading, different in
Other times
Where words
Renewed by stone, red mud,
White mask, feathered keep
Flying urgency, oh, oh
A longing to
Speak!
Aching mute
A river surge
Swelling silent

So many thoughts
Roosting in night trees
Like unseen call
From lost bird
Finding voice

One day soon

One morning before awake
A dark bruised bird flew through glass
Ignored your white circles of salt
Stole the sleeping tongue in your mouth
And left before sun had completed rising

All day you watched ribbons of felt break across clouds like dazed dancers
Unsure of their next footfall
Brittle cicadas droning out breeze and riddles

Where light ends, dying over violet
Night breathed deeply in a thought
As elastic fish swam upriver defying
Consolations, winking with ignited
Temper

Many times a wolf would miss howl, owl their hoot, silence a rain of peace
Lighting cooling against tarmac after
Heavy warm rain, I need not voice or
Artifice

Settlement in fog

I just dropped something
But I don't know what it was
A sound like a thin nail
Or penny
Maybe the edge of
Today
Or life
Inside shattered glass
Peering through jagged
Trying to find
Settlement in fog

No, and no and not

Strong enough?
To hold down
Thrashing weakly
A dying cat
Strong enough
Heart laboring in empty chest
Filling sink
Imagining
When you plunge
Life in agony
Prevent further pain
Drowning quickly
What will you feel?
Gentle goodbye, cool water
Vivid color no smell
Loosening, reaching, keening
When does life extinguish?
And death replace
I loved you so much
Giving me strength
No, weakness, no, murder
Thinking of the *Grimm's* fairy-tail
Girl holds a key to forbidden room
Apple on tree
Bible echoes even for unbelievers
You took a life, you saved a life?
Was it yours to take?
She was suffering
We're all suffering
Was it yours to make?
If not now then when?
Why at all
Why not? Thin lines
(euthanasia, when is it too much?)
(or not enough?)
She drowned in a pillow cover
Unconsciously red
As I lifted her head

Heavy in snapped death
(how fast it happens)
(you were alive warm, now not)
Water crimson
Dye from fabric or me?
Blood on my hands
Smell in bed
One pillow cover less
Did I set her free?
(feeble clay we are by what right?)
(even if there is no Maker in the sky)
Story girl, palm marked by key
What is allowed, what is sin?
Everyone knows what she's done
Banished till a prince comes
(apple falling, was a pomegranate)
(bite, or not, sin patient in naught)
There's no mark, no stain, and yet
Where she is buried I see only red
Earth, tears, regret

My hands

My hands held life
They comforted the dying swallow fallen from her nest
Willing her to live, knowing her rapid heart would slow
My hands caressed your face, outlines playing against outlines
A silhouette of fancy
Our bodies melted
Fingers scented
Caught in hair
Sticking to each other
Like love lorn seals
Warm against the cold
My hands now prematurely old
Bloodied by what has passed
Life, choices, death, the still heart
No more, words crumble
Red hands wiped and still
Stains of conscience, mercy and convenience
Keeping wakeful like harvest moon
Shines awake the heavy sleeper
Wrapping secrets in gauze
Drowning their beseeches
Walking as if you had control
over anything, even death

Oreo

Not a bronze girl on marble step
Inverted, sandaled feet and hiked skirt
Thighs brown like sun tea
Youth's elixir fishing in cool water
No time obliterates freedom
Felt in fine bleached hairs
Catching light on her arm
Careless in existing without effort
Oleander and pomegranate
In shadows I listen, seas briny call
Grinding foam underfoot, wild,
Unyielding in cats eyes, rushing
To gather my pale limbs, rejected
Strange in contrast, albino in
Shade, reddening with humidity
Waiting for suns release from
Sky, falling like velvet curtains
A silent edict closing day
Birds quiet in burnished trees,
Glittering night squalls diving
Now I exist brightly, shimmering
In mirrored water, an opal echoing
Moonlight tattooing pallor with
Confident brush stroke
Mandala Oreo

Fever Girl

Fever; is a girl's voice over phone
When blurred crickets trip heals
Questions of identity asked by strangers
Where were you born? What do you know?
Haunch the horse helmet, not Greeks
Nor a condom called *Trojan*
Fever isn't bullish, nor ram, it isn't saying no but taking yes
Willows dip low, bow to questions
Don't drink from the stamen
Jeopardize clouded girls powdering
Their ready hymens
Blood in rivers, baskets empty of prophet
Blackbirds song from deep in thicket
Fever is mint and lemon,
Water run over rock
Wear the mantle
Find jewels in river stone
Walk over me, leave prints
Leave me eternally thirsty
Henna enjoining, long roads
Seasoned by wild thyme
It is burgundy and permanent
Her hands hot on white linen
Bursting in silent furnace
fever dreams of molten
And caught static breath
Straining against dawn

Love's symmetry

Why does she love her so much
Why her?
Too many jostling elbows and unwashed feet
Crammed into cabs, computer screens, art events, peep shows, wedding cakes
Why pick anyone?
Choosing lollipops in alternate colors
Sliding your tongue over each and other
Her call, her brand of perfume, this dissuaded circle of hair staining the empty bottom of
your unused life
Take a number, pitch a scene, write yourself in
Tongue a stranger, silver and blue, music in motion, tears in pages flipped through
Why anyone? Why you?
And still the kitchen clock ticks
Mice as yet discovered tiptoe
Her arm languid in sleep
A bunched fist, dreaming cheek
Breasts too soft to stay in place
The mystery of time and space
A smell in the crook of her neck
Reminding you of then and yet...
Why and not, play fellows, dark eyed doe
Fireflies outside flickering
Night's hush and serene close

Wonderment in emptiness

When I think about sex
After all men
Sleeping standing up
The woman or girl I invite
To my internal dialogue
What if my ass wasn't sinking and anything was possible
Would I?
Try you out for size?
Develop strategies?
Confidence over cocktails
Different skin, shades, colors
Find out what all the fuss is about
Men using bathroom breaks to jerk off
Every six minutes
Thinking about sex
I've never understood that
Hole in the mentality
Where's love? Joy in familiarity?
Happiness is found in variation
My eyeballing men folk say
Not tired repetition, a man's
Born to breed or slide
in anything that opens
Not picky just pricky
Us cunts we like to stay
And find our joy in more than
A crack at, or triple digit
Wonderment in emptiness

Careful!

Candy! Pick up your toys
That's not how you grease a pan
Careful! Don't go hurtling past!
What did you do to your new dress? It's all covered in mud!

Bull in a china shop
Born to careful folk
Their house clean enough for unexpected guests
No kicking under the bed or hasty spit wiping windows here

Dishes washed grouting scrubbed
When polishing silver, dip just so
Shining shoes a five step process carefully lay paper down, no marks

Painting cupboards divide the area off
Sand down surface using rough then fine grained paper
Don't be sloppy, training precision
Sparkling, clean, neat, tidy, everything in place

Candy wears her dragon costume
Careful to hide her tail underneath
A bird's nest of tangled hair
Drags her largest teddy to the wigwam
Fashioned from blankets and clothes hangers

A mess, peaceful inside like *Stig In The Dump*
Light reflecting through her grandmother's sole attempt at patchwork
She was clean too, Freda's vacuum music she turned the volume up and drank, going over
already pristine carpet

Candy isn't the same, she always made a mess, didn't mean to, she's too far in her head
Where clouded mirrors and lurking dust balls play with smudges on the walls
And toys talk and dreams walk and nothing is ordered except nightfall

Seasonal attachment

Attachments are baubles
Sometimes they catch and fall,
Fine glass shards, caught in pine needles, getting between toes, why didn't we buy a fake tree again?
Others, fare well, higher in branches
Impervious to bulky Winter coats brushing past, they know to endure, to last.
Ephemeral, catching light from apparent dark, seemingly other worldly,
We find ourselves looking, then again, becoming familiar with, like rain against glass,
soothes a sleeper, and sounds below conscious thought play long in dream

Silence in the house at three

Jasmine and wild honeysuckle
June bugs amble through lilac
We are from this place, our hands
Bear marks from its walls
Prints against cold tile, feet
Still running up stairs, gripping banisters, the whelp and warp
Sharp splinters, iodine, there, there, all better now.

Brother, sinew and tan, eyes same shape as mine, darker, seeing past
Intolerable, clasping my fingers until they cramp, pulling me out of my head
Keep moving, don't quit and let spiders in, no time for dawdle, now we grow
Watch us keen against late sun, itching
At our bones, long and lean like sleeping cats, hunting against the garden wall, a smell of
bonfire and cinder

Pin wheeling arms, autumn color, small of damp brick and dew caught in webs
I never want to go home, your hot breath in my ear, wax and wane, two who are one and
same, looking at you, a mirror in rain

Dry drunk

Take a girl like you
Underneath feathers not much ado
Three generations of drunks
Ends in my lap
Ironically last of us
And I'm dry as dusty walls
Tiny pinpricks showing light
A colander bodice leaking sobriety

Why don't I climb on a stool
Perfect poise, pointed toes, tuck chin,
Arc and flip, dive right in?
My lovers are all soaks of one type

Rummy eyed, slight eight pm slur, hell, often by three
Shaking hands, fragile bones, strong stomachs
Honesty from a bottle, constant companion, I the declining nurse, getting off on what?
Vicarious thumbing
Noses at convention, sweet profanities, arguable loss of control, indecent sexual appetite?

If I were half sauced I'd have the courage to answer for my tastes, turn my clothes inside
out, wear my scars and angered rosettes to town
But this is your dress rehearsal, your play, a finery of broken things still shining,

I like my role, picking up rags, stuffing my mouth with combustibles, eating pieces of fatty
liver; evermore a drinker of other's exploring chaos from the safety of theater's rafters

Hot gun

He slings guns like burgers
In noon day heat
Where lizards turn to yolk
If too long on the road
Curled into dried cusps

He packs his head with stories
False prophets and tired churches
Gasping for attention, told him
SIN, impregnates our best intent
Better learn to oil your resolve son

At 21 his father buys him a gun
Equipped with a certainty of youth
Under full yellow moon, cicadas
Dying and mating in masks
His best expression, parody

Though a bullet traveling fast
Eclipses a runner, this is only practice
For his own end, rounding itself
On blunt attempt at vigor
Where burnt sun meet high tree

The traits of my race; Rachel Dolezal

Rachel wearing *Laura Ashley*
Blonde and blue
White as Anglo milk on rye
I'll take your race and divide and divide
Parents thought so too
Rachel wasn't entirely true

Bathe in chestnuts
Ink your skin
Weave secrets in hair
And lint in your grin

Rachel married a man of many colors
Birthed a child of coffee and tea
Got an education in equality
And the strife of those not white
Like Rachel's blonde and blue type

At some shaken juncture
Armed with wig and paint
She leapt from porcelain's shelf
And embraced her inner fake

Rachel are you Black? Are you White?
Does it matter when day is night?
She girded her best attempts with
Actor's bravado
Who would doubt the disciplines
Of a dark and light marvel?

Maybe now, it's splashed in print
Your life, your gamble, your invented in
Colors our assumptions, our best kept
Lies, who we want to be, where secrets
Hide.

Rachel, girl of opaque, torn down
She turned herself from white to brown
And with those curls, that affect, maybe real
Her blood as red as judgment's zeal
Color is, and is not, a measure, a cast
But who really knows the shades of another's heart?

By anyone and by nothing

Stop tasting; stop seeing
Remove clothes not of your making
Thinner, thinner, till it's gone
An ache in place of nothing hard won

There is something deep down ugly
About the way you look at me
As if life had been swallowed from your eyes
And turning back they stare at me
Opaque in marble, washed of care

If I could scrub my conscience clean
With my own torn heart
Still the damage remains
Written across us like fireworks
Hardening concrete, maturing bark
Something permanent containing
The stain

You can try to suffocate the air
Or win a moment in hours of dying
White flowers, heads drowsy
These only bring mirrors closer
Reflecting identical outcomes
All savaged by empty eyes
Blind to redemption

There's nobody watching
Steal a kiss, smoke my fate
All color leaches when sunlight
Fighting on horizon loses
To dark inevitable fancies
And I, I know you left your heart
To be swallowed whole
By anyone and by nothing

Half cocked

The internet opened a path to ugliness
Sure, the world was sporadically cutthroat before
But like the murdered who are not found
Such grotesques stayed for the most part obscured

Digital gave our withered hearts skates with knives
Whizzing at impossible speed a gallery of the absurd
We flung our former privacies spread legged and juicy
"Notice me! Touch my fantasies, adulterate my tedium!"

The world became a collective caw of self, self, self
Brimming with illusionistic grandeur, losing shame by the pound
We cancan like painted parrots for the public Selfie
Delving for reality, a doll house of half written stories

Soon, our fingerprints were lost to manic cyber fucking
A Roman mass of reconstitute
Children pretending to be college professors
Men masturbating to hens laying kittens
50 year old Welsh farmer's posing as Brazilian lesbians

And in the real world, coffee is getting worse, you can't find a decent cotton shirt, chocolate
is mixed with *Teflon* and nobody worries who left the lights on.

My faithless

Goodbye you
Place of seven memories
How soon your walls empty
Of our shared time
When others put posters, masks, photographs
I will have whitened out
A chalky figure
Indistinct
Just one among many
To call you home

Artificial appetites

Artifice you beguile me
Two for one vibrators
YouTube on your wrist
24 hour live streaming
Check the pets and the kids

Artifice you destroy me
Sex over love with sell by dates
Perishable plastic families
impermanence is our queen
Emptiness becomes art

Auditioning patience

Faith is a lizard sunning on stucco
Breeze compels his neck to swell
Coral is the swell, stark against green
What does he think? As he bobs to dip and preen

Loss is a white house empty of love
Pieces of you thrown on a cold hearth
Roses curling thorns around my neck
Who will speak? Cause birds to break formation, filling sky with heckle

Solace is a cold river, pine needles and wild sage, broken calls of kiting hawks gaming indecisive clouds
A dripping tap rusts, coppery water wakes us, we rise, we fall, we resume

Haunted ambelic

A house is not a home
Home; what then constitutes
A place of safety and repose?

Reassurance in numbers?
Rows of incubators
Jaundiced newborns

Welcome; a land of inequalities
Random or purposeful?
Pluck an apple eat a maggot

You went with Parent A
I stayed waiting for Parent B
Who perennially late had missed
His bus

You had a house with shuttered doors
Secrets brewing in heavy broth
Thick coated impossible dogs
Pulling everything out of joint

I found rooms of silence heaped upon
Magnified terror dancing in tandem
To sounds of shut doors, listening
Fur coats laden with collected dust

We met at playschool
Not choosing pursuit of mindless tag
Already aware we were caught
In fine untenable webs of heredity

In the library I exposed my scabs exchange for boiled sweets
books our vessel's, feet claimed in shoes forming premature calluses

Parent A gave you unconditional love and unhealthy food
Parent B forgot and I walked home
Through empty parks where I left dreams to build castles without me

You grew up complete, I a little splintered
Home, just a suitcase for past
Once closed it exists in recollection
A spell able to alter memory

I chose to live in trees, you among lions
Indefinitely postponing maturity
And that urge to call anywhere ours
Such places are phantom solace for souls without doors.

For Johann.

Grief and the beautiful girl with tattoos

Grief they say
Is catching
I never found this to be true

People cross the road whispering;
"There's the daughter whose papa passed
I don't know what to say!"

The beautiful tattooed girl
Came to work missing her father
Like light; he was gone, to die

Her colleagues tiptoed crane-esque
Unsure of words, hesitant to touch
Her burning shoulders

She was a seraphim as yet unawares
Wings folded on sorrows keep
Tattooed with molten grief

Her father had always known
From his early bed of soil, rose
Her wings enveloped, in scattered milagro sigh

One day when earth turned closer
To the sun
She lifted from the ground
And like starlight, shone

Illusions of existing

Deeply curtseyed cut a bow
Sweating roses lights behind sheen
All of time has come and passed
In this little epoch this little farce

Still in the thrall
Driving violent thunder
Cars as slim as your cigarette
Powder dreams without release
You blow, you spasm, you exist
For that flickering eclipse

Lover, mother, child, suffer
Edging out of rain your feet are webbed
Polished on the souls of fallen
A fire dancer its embers becoming jewels
Too much in one heart for truth

The Waxen Effigy and the Real Estate Agent

What would happiness look like?
Typically verbose I stood mute
Worse than an answer I didn't want to give
Or a lie I refused to make
The truth was bald and wordless
A maggot without a mouth
I couldn't answer because I didn't have an answer
Days later learning about telomeres
I wondered if the real estate agent
Still talked to her husband
Her banana yellow outfits and social smile
Were things I admired and simultaneously reviled
If my telomeres shorten will I grow forgetful
And not remember I still owe an answer
Or that the world needs decorating
And participation is mandatory

It's a Socialist Jewish thing

A gay Jew with no family and a mistrust of authority hears that their childhood friends
think Israel is guilty of war crimes
The gay Jew with no family had a communist grandparent and considers the ideals of
socialism to be more legitimate in theory than capitalism
Despite contradicting that with a recent urge to support the death penalty in a few select
cases
And possibly a growing affection for restrictions on immigration numbers
As one herself and also left handed she wore an eye patch for a lazy eye for several years as
a child
Whilst her best friend at school was married off at nine and sent to Pakistan
It's not skin color determining her belief immigration needs control its lack of
cohesiveness, jobs and future
Maybe isolationism, the polar opposite of her socialist ideals isn't such a bad idea?
And whilst she loves her neighbors six kids she did read; *The Population Bomb*
If Israel weren't so hot she may go, though some shiksa she'd make with no womb or family
tree, not even an olive branch
But her cynicism is really just loss though whose loss she is perplexed
Whilst people have multiple births and who knows? In 20 years father's may marry
daughters and join cults or live on Mars, and if so, could there be an Israel on Mars? Or will
we all be flying rabbits in the next life? Eating nectarines and *Hamburger Helper*?

Lie to me

Empty words oh empty words
How did you capture my attention?
So certain of cynicism despite this I opened up like a book without a story hungry for blank
pages to fill with lies
No real explanation
Not for those muddled trusts and trysts of teen years
Nor furtive hope of rekindled passion later on
How surely can I be so gullible if I see the game? If I know the moves?
Why if treachery is a wound I peer into often
Would your comfortable lies fit neatly against my heart?
Or invariably when they produce no blood
The stone squeezed dry of fakery
Am I surprised at my aptitude
For believing again, those empty lies?

At least we are all alien

Nobody wants to visit me
The neighbor too loud plays her TV
I've seen life on this planet and that's why I'm looking elsewhere

They say its racist here, color counts
All action is distilled into screaming headlines
I wasn't sure I had skin before I heard it on the radio
Thinking back is that why they wouldn't serve me ice cream?

You won't come and prove me wrong
Though Denmark has an equal history and let's not get started on Italy....
Everywhere is racist, everyone could be
Or color could stop shouting and visit

But as a queer walking down the streets bare chested and gnashing for change
Reluctantly I agree and wonder
How expensive will it cost to meet on Mars?

Dead bird

It's just a dead bird
Why bury it?
So the other children ran at the sound of the bell ending playtime
Was my staying past, when it began?
Charmed into rebellion by a dead birds glassy eyes?
If the Thames river flooded, the bird would drift with silt
The school would submerge in brackish waters
Our paintings a momentary color
Our memories irrelevant
No grave for birds or wayward children who stay beyond the bell
Where bodices confines cannot snatch their longing to climb trees instead of sums or
graphs or modes of etiquette
For why must we wash? Or avoid barbed wire? When all your words are sharpened with
the sadness of being grown?
And I am free
Free to make boats of banyan trees and briar moss, to fill my sleeves with raspberries and
starlight and climb the beanstalk
The dead gaze of the bird, washed over and made new, made silver
We climb high, we watch the children line up to be counted, sit down to be indoctrinated,
sip insipidly the ripe milk of snack time and fill their bellies with swill
We are free, we are not here, we are among the dreamers in the earth and sky, where
nothing lives and nothing dies

The Father figure

What did they make of you?
Gasping middle age wrapping unforgiving around slack stomachs
Did they want to feed on your crisp unexpected availability?
Fight amongst themselves, cats, pigeons?
Did this make you billy goat? Ram? Or snake?
Though surely as they were edging closer
You reeled them
Knowing as they could never, sensing as desperation blinds those who stricken by urges
flounder
All the while, a perfect gentleman surrounded by panting hens
It embarrassed me, not your disregard once you used and flung aside the lucky
But their heaving heterosexuality
Burgeoning with last chance sex, second families, children over 40, dresses that his stretch
marks
It wasn't the aim but the production, a bosomy race to gain
What? I knew you had no heart to give and you knew it too
Only they, putting aside sense *en mass* and puffing their chests in pursuit
Were blind to a futility and your seamless guile

Past tense present absent

Exhausted rain tired of falling
Mottled walls beige and boring
Stare through smoke find your mom
She's the one she's the one

Breasts with scars lips without
Words can't hurt said the mouthless cunt
Eat you eat me devour our aches
Spit the seeds to mate with saints

Born in fire in oil in gravy
Slide out fast before love gets lazy
Thrust and purge semen smelling sheets
Reminds us of childhood of secrets of treats

Your bow my arrow fingers in the pie
Delve too deep make the virgin cry
Shatter ghosts the past reveals naught
Except on Sunday when flagellation is taught

Crouching in mud daub me a river
Catching fish like you held my nipple
Slippery fast maybe it never happened
In water everything is different
Even color even cake even the sounds drowning children make

Compulsion's riddle

It is commonly thought, compulsion has some source
Surely, say the Well Adjusted People of Pleasant
Nothing so wild can come a burning without a trail?
There must, an ember uprooted, some cause for this rot?
If we are, as The Good Folk believe, born without taint
Lying in bassinet, halo and crucifix twin set
How, astounded, the crestfallen wobbling might of morality says

I know, this riddle and more
The choke on that barking dog
His collar strangling
A savagery blinking within
He forgets he loved
He longs to be free
Even as night gives way to dark thoughts

A burning road is carefully hewn
From sedate, sensible appearance
The chair of judgment becomes throne
And a dormant switch
That lay undiscovered entire lives
Casts shadows never breathed before
One moment, we are ourselves
One moment we are maw
Lurching tunnel of capture
Roaring from familiar like dry grass
Catching flame and rising silently
out of nothing into all we ever were

Twin

Born in the same bed
From different wombs
Our blood mixed together
Before we knew
In my hours before you
I waited without cry
Less than a day passed
And you joined me then, now and every time since
My double, the shade in shadow
You fill me with love
Every time I'm reminded
We were born in a bed
That's where we lay
I was born first
And I waited for you all day.

For Johann

Mercurial

Steady hunger transforming
Until eating is an externality
Foreign like being touched
When last was I in your arms
Tight against your chest
Inseparable yet I cleave
Far from you in my misery

Your hands in mine

If your fingers let go
Rain dissecting vision in summer downpour
Turning clarity to mud
If I walk home
Every step further from you
Feet high in bleached grass
Curious flowers staining ankles
If then we had never and all was dream
I would keep walking into the earth
Calling without your tongue for this
Abandoned segment of my heart
Silver under moonlight
Burning at the fringes of memory
Even if you never returned
My feet would make sand walking
Until voices that grow without light
Would echo in my blind forage
Through wall and sea I'd break
My own making and turn to wing
Vibrating on your shore for that rain
And rising tides of you beating me flat
Bringing me back, a somersault of
Wordless violet, we begin and end
In the strength of your hands in mine
For all of time

Rabbit Heart

Over the mauve sun
Releasing into smudges of green
Blurred landscapes of sleeping magic
The rabbit ran
Her heart a violent echo
Kept with agitated pace
She looked into the far distance
Hoping to smell like approaching rain
A way forward
Releasing her yoke from physical
To a light footed spirit world
Where all she had ever loved
In that too fast heart
Waited with happy eyes
To see once again
Her home, where she belonged
And not this long chalky road of tears
Of surviving against harshly
Constructed cities
Left her aching to escape
And feel again, soft grass under foot
Without a racing tired heart
Urging its last flight
Seeing only sharpness
Cutting air like a sheaf
Without purpose

The uterus is surgically absent

What becomes of the fallen?
Biting tongues to appear worthy
Illusion of strength
White teeth, no cavities allowed
Visible perfection
Bunions to the back
Hide yourself in falsehood
Dancing so fast to keep your position in the line
One slip, one moment of sense, one truism
And the play house shuts its doors
Bolts the lock and eats the key
You're outside now
Where skies seem dimmer
This time if you fall
If the babies aren't born
If you woke with nothing at all
That absent heart
Quiet in a thundering chest
Will turn to thorns
Prick you inside out
Turn skin to hide
Burn safety in salute
Of absent friends and
Board games missing pieces

No Memory of the ocean

Youth reflects love as perfection
We haven't yet lived together
Meeting for dates, chosen like scenes
From favorite movies
A bench by the river at night
Moon lighting our kisses
Hands entwined in rapid fumble
Sex between the buttons
We don't know then
Time is an exploding force
One day you notice your first gray
And I find a disquieting unsettlement
Gazing in place of you
A dysmorphic shift from lust
To panicked love, the moving van, the first coat of paint
Fingerprinted hours
Shoplifted memories, cataract silence
A bruise where my heart polka danced
Worse than absence is the gradual shift to indifference
White feathers on the floor, something spilt and flying
Love is an arc, leaving you talking to strangers more than each other
A loneliness specific to company like
Sardines without oil, gasping in tin
They dry until in pieces flake
Only the impression of having existed
No memory of the ocean remains

Leaching life from the tallest

You know how MANTRA dictates
repeat Positivism's
And they will come to pass
Like a seed sown turns into a hardy oak
Except
Seeds also
Rot, calcify, get irrevocable diseases, plain ole die or fail to thrive
The dwarfism of the seed is the inability we have
As towering infernos of rapture and piss
To see the lunacy of our mutant egos
Failing to understand the pattern of downfall
Witnessing in slow motion, there's one year, there's another
I don't recognize this way Mama
Even the moon turns yellow
My best attempt at reinvention
Among the leaves watching itself fail to become
Even that weed you half admire before destroying

The reluctance of endurance

I don't want the phone to ring. Ever.
I don't want reminders of love splatter don't want to exist in this face, this case
This voice, this endless race, this burning bed, this empty head
I cannot ask when they held my funeral
It was too long ago to remember like it was always there just around the corner
Seeing color leach from my face
Every blanched moment
A montage of mistakes beginning with birth
I never asked for it I cried, then, now, forever
I never asked for any of it
And that is why it was always wrong
Not just now or then but inevitably eternally
Because sometimes you aren't meant to
And still, you do
Endure
Long after everything you tried to make it stop
Fell away like old bandages
Leaving you raw under the spotlight of irony

Tight symmetry

A failure lived in a tower of feathers
In what's supposed to be the driest time of year it rained roses
Give up your dead, leave them to propagate
Why play poker when leaves turn red in trees?
Fly, or fall, abject or...
This season, that last glance, the rain was so heavy, so full, cutting out sound
I saw you mouth word, whatever said, lost in a hum
Falling water through crying air, sodden
Absence before the break sets in
No preservatives, we last until
The final drop, when voices ash to earth
How about later? How about breaking open and seeing the seeds, in all their tight symmetry?

Eclipsed detach

Disconnect
Trace
Your skin over screens
Blinking light
Energy eating time
Trace
I send myself in a gif
You receive an approximated
Flicker of real
Swap for one second
Of holding hands
Proper
Or is that old school
Like phones that dial through
And connect us
Voices then now screens
Soon a figure in ether?
Fall in love two brains in a jar?
Trace
I can't say it isn't real
But what if nothing is
Not this, not that, not all
This game of catch
Where souls lose in eclipsed detach

All the time in the world

The girl in a dark jacket reminded me of a dried vulture
Her angry raisin eyes bore through my thin defense
I hadn't come to party, I'd forgotten how to smile
I was wearing my sensible knickers and my greyed bra
Even though they tell you have good matching underwear
In case you get run over and the fireman or medic is a hottie
The absurdity when uniforms only belied a soul wanting to be obedient
I never liked the boxed and ready route
If I'd been male I'd have chewed my tie and ripped away the artifice
To bloom in wild nectar and defy rule
But as a girl I hid behind long hair, the false smile
Wondering when I'd see you, why you'd asked
I trembled to think of the moment our eyes would lock. I wanted that moment. I ran from it.
Like an old friend though, inevitably, the anxiety defused and I knew you
These years haven't tarnished that memory at all since
I can stand there, back cold against the wall, eyes wide and searching
Until through the throng of gladdened bodies merging, you could be picked out by the
brightness in your eyes
Strange for eyes so dark, I recall thinking, and so, they glowed like your desire for me, a
bushel of unsaid things on fire, lighting the darkness with expectation and fear
All I could think about were your hands and whether they would be inside me
If the words as yet uttered would ever be admitted and how your arms would feel around
me without clothes, because no time has yet been long enough for me to ever know

Girl of the sky

Water a cactus to hasten its rot
Once lush and protected
Bloated and mauve
I tried to revive you in the desert
my pink heels gave me no leverage
We scooped out your life
From wane suitcases pealing
I folded you inside, *muneka*, paper rose
Leaving no room for your clothes
They blew in unfurling ribbons
red were streaks
On distant Joshua trees
Yoking the setting sun with filament
Of faraway caravans heavy in unison
We buried your diaries, photos and hair
Underneath the moon when light scattered
You were just a shadow
No corn, no voice
We danced nearly together by fire light
And cactus fever
Until the circle our feet made
Wore a brilliant orange glow
And I saw you before you left
Smiling over your shoulder
Made of stars
You were gone with daybreak
Like dew even in the hottest places
Can be found and transforms
Into sky

French for tongue

What do I do if only one of us notices anything and only one of us speaks?
How do I mend fences with half of us?
With this, which says it's us, so incomplete?

Turning orange

I find it must be a perverse cruelty when we met you said how could anyone stand not to touch me for years? You didn't understand, it perplexed your notion, as passion licked your heels for my mouth.
and now, unwrapping the end of fire, I appreciate the same way you can make yourself bleed and feel release, that strong loves are moths, they burn up in their captive light

Mercurial, fucked in the head, or just thinking?

I could easily be out of it all the time. Ironically I never am but I want to be. Just like how I felt so sexual but didn't have sex in years. Weird to be one way but live another. Suppose a choice is better than a prison? Though prison is within the trapped heart of a fighter who lost. I don't understand mercurial dreams. I could be a nympho or a nun just as easily such contradictory things dual within me and as sad as I always am I can roar with laughter and be so excited and then so dead inside. The only constant is mistrust and love of saying good night and climbing in bed

Without my interjection

In other words you create a stage
and I walk onto it
but I wasn't the instigator
of what u came away feeling
(that I don't love you)
you were
Chicken and egg
which came first?
Both unwittingly sabotage now
a self-fulfilling prophecy
We return to it maddeningly
Castrated cocks fighting
Not bloody more empty pecks
Everything that gave us fire
Burned off
Leaving charred circles
Taunting the embrace
Of a play with endless words
And no conclusion

That's like having a glass heart

Where can living just for the moment ever grow?
An ugly facsimile of what could have been
Haunted echo of lost hope
Place of no sanctuary that cannot express itself with a constraint of imposed restriction
And that is why we watch it die
Like having a glass heart.

What do I know?

What do I know?

Do I know you?

Do you know yourself?

Masks are more honest

They hide what we pretend we don't want to hide

Those fixtures in our hearts

The people we love

Perhaps just one

Perhaps love can only stand to love once

A stain that changes DNA

Becomes as much us as not us

Stranger to us

Part of

An eclipse leaving us in darkness

Bringing us only light

How can I want to die

If I love and how can I live

If not

If not you

Positioned in naught

Do you remember the feeling of being safe?
Tucked up in your car seat
Given free toys by smiling faces
A bed with thick cotton and rabbits
Baths that became oceans
You carried me on your hip
The warmth of your skin, the softness of your hair
Or did I carry you?
Not hip but inside, a longing like hunger
You were not there in the shadows
Nor standing in the doorway with light spilling through
You were not there for breakfast or the reduced days
As our cupboard grew empty our world shrunk
We stopped talking, we learned not to want to try
Language was survival
Water cold and shallow
Everything wasn't
You weren't
And I wasn't sure you ever had been
Though somewhere on me, I still, carry the feeling, that you were.

Cocoon

I am holding on
Bound by thick finger
Attached with hope
If it rains I may dissolve
Sink into earth
To begin all over
A patience without mind
This just happens
Or storms will rip my moorings
To fly in night and slow dream
I may open not where I start
But far in unfamiliarity
Where emerging I find
Others born in strange places
With no landmark of how we came
To twist in cloud, gather in dust
And landing, split and release
All our waiting
All we are and will be

Expected

If you were never here
I would still be unborn
Expectant on conception's valley
So close to breath but
It took your forging through
Torments and time until
You asked for me into the night
An echo you thought unheard
I began that very moment
To grow closer to life
As if waiting forever
I had learned you inside out
Or was, that part making us both
Whole only when together
You knew something was wrong
All those days apart it felt strange
Until from your own self I came
Expectant
Neither new nor old
Just yours

Who leaves behind

Who
Leaves behind
Promises like confetti
Scattered
My arms ache
An empty place between
Where you were
Folded close to my heart
Now
Windows flung carelessly
Raw sea breezes and mocking
Wielding birds higher than sight
Feet raw with sand
Nothing else
Even night cusps against moon
Trying not to disturb
A hush fallen on this place
Since you took the words
Left hollow shells
Paving roads in water
leading only deeper
Where nobody returns whole
As if never, touch or sound
Existed in more than memory
As fine as dried salt
Caught on the hem of everything
Leaching a little color
With each rinse

Yellow circles

All in yellow circles
A day's work, begun in earnest
Watching for the peak of day
Lines of sun webbing the water
Reflections of directions never taken
Her straining stomach wrapped in hope
His eyes creased by squinting at the future
Chalk marks the spot
Her heals indent the grass
Digging deep into succulence
She's not running if she's coming back
Though you never catch her
The loop is fixed and repeating
Try as you might there's no way
To penetrate circles left long in rain
Filling with time, once and again
Shell be someone else next time you meet
Perhaps have your frown and you her earth stained feet

Coming up for air

Do you remember the smell of blue leather polish? We'd cover our scuffed sensible school to go out bright and hidden

the splinters in adventure playgrounds were always sharper than sour cola bottle treats devoured

sitting on flat garage roofs, facing weeds and plants with thin pink flowers that smelt like cat piss

sometimes when you weren't there, I'd dissect a plant, watch the seeds spill onto the gravel

there was a world inside the flower, all the parts had a function you couldn't tell by looking

this ordinary weed containing all the segments for life.

long hours waiting after school for my father to turn the road on his bike, the uncomfortable ride home

maybe a treat of polish sausage or Chinese bun hidden with his ink pens slung across his back

apt to forget I needed picking up, faster than any car, oblivious to my interior life

like those who watched the weeds and thought nothing of them or how their roots grew ever more

under the yielding concrete of broken houses and interrupted fortress games written in chalk

only you and I climbed the sticky tree to the garage roof to see the world the way it really hung, sharp and crumbling

did he know we fell into the cold water like stones, and sinking, the teacher would yell; "Find the brick on the bottom!" I would dive, smelling underwater which they say isn't possible, watching light eat darkness just a little, and the echoes of a verruca socked world stagnating above

I wanted to swim beyond the brick, or have it tow me under, to the silvery places in my books, or some high roof top, where even weeds couldn't reach and despair couldn't creep

but we always broke the surface around the same time, you'd laugh that I forgot the brick but it was always deliberate, I wanted to save it from coming up for air.

Plastic swimming caps

Perhaps she was an acrobat not chicken skin diving

past the taunts the laughs who cares if British Home Stores

makes the worst swimming costumes because when you

reach the highest plank and feel the wobble against your human hands

what's possible in the air a flame, a dragon, a fantasy

out of here, out of the smell of chlorine the shriek of boys pushing girls

pushing boundaries plugging up holes with tampons and tea bags

what's it all about when your horse is waiting outside and you can run

so fast lungs burning smelling piss in the grass and the dank skies over head

council estates like vultures looming you'll end up in one

with a cat and a tin of spam on three legs and drunk in

that cage rattling until the rabbit is freed he runs ahead of every

greyhound who isn't fed enough to really give a shit

diving as elegantly as stars falling through high clouds

for that second you're a mermaid surrounded in silver

drowning out curses and cruelty, seeing only splendor

dreams as bright and lovely as the feeling of warm clothes

on a hot day, steam rising from the school radiator we'd sit

banging our calves on the metal pushing each other noticing

peeling paint, wax on the wood, splinters of time

thinking about it thirty years later, still diving

far far into space

The hour collapses willingly upon us

Green buds, their raw urging

emerge in crowns of soil

cleaving recalcitrant clay,

sharp figures of lit tallow

burning through prospecting ink

on my way to you

Our elbows raw from kneading at dawn

bread rises with secrets curled in Night's veil

knees ache over cold stones; unyielding prayer

however many fire flies exist in a jar

are but glimmers against eyes without sight

You feel the hush of a sleeping place

though you have quenched dreams long before

instead tracing imagined towers in fog

wakeful and exhausted; love pouring over still form

as rivers of wild bloom effloresce

Darkness glints, distant ember

blue and green life marled into rope

fragile climb bending at the neck

what witness of inner life's nectar fall?

Where then is your hand to clasp?

birds over sea; a mirror and sky; glass

where do I place my cold heart?

To return, color of highland, untamed moment

long held, damp smile reaching pinched starlight

remembered by cusped pressure; silver moons

Your fingers circling my wrists, holding steady.

Hiroshima 70

With bow and silver arrow
Gods woke
From ore
Shattering crimson flagstones
I heard bombs drop
Like daisy flowers

Outside turned inside as
Explosion pealed trees raw
children made white with parents ash, ran burning streets, besmeared in coin of gore

We called this an end to hostilities
Carving revenge in plumes of smoke
As the bomb released, graceful fell, an origami lantern of many colors, flickering behind
charred retina

Proud of our bouquet, delivering
Radian death by cowards embrace
Our submarines tucked beneath ocean swallowed shame, cinders in retreat
Pretending in absence, we hadn't really done this, if distanced from the thing enough, a
little less, culprit

All souls are immortal in history
Reward comes in morning
White birds turning red
Crossing from life
Japan sighed in weight of death
Flag in circled blood, bore rising sun

Remember. Hiroshima.

Water

It's a place dresses doused in glitter, made from light
fit just right
acceptance comes served in New Year cheer
fizzing over sincere
you're okay as you are, bring yourself raw
this is a table of love
carved on the walls are stories of all the steps
we took a long time yes
when time stops and shakes her head in mirth
at all you've gained and lost
this meal will fill your empty hollows
and smiles so abundant they'll multiply
into pieces of moon cut out glass and stone
hanging over hollows where light never grew
holding hands in fitful glee stepping closer
we hold our hands to the fire, we leap

The Devil's Instant (or an ode to hating small talk)

Talk that size is cheap
Masks in masks
Profit from varnish
Fish wives, baker's dozen
Chitter chatter
Telegraph gossip

Reverent evil
In everyday soup
I ate my greens
Can I leave the table
Now?

A barrel of school custard
I'd rather try to digest
Than elevator muzak
Playing repeat
On station phony

Inadequate blood supply
Drill small holes
Let flow
See more,
Thinking in waves

Your heads wear
Cellophane hats
Gags
Party favors
Unwitting guest
Stays a year
Drones in my ear
No season of cheer

You need to be quiet
Or speak when spoken to
Children in cupboards
With content leaking through

Did you want us
To grow up?
Be just like you?
Bee hive and fondue?

Blaming socialization
On tedious quip
Cease talk of short kind
Re-make, re-define
Laundry list

Baby's first tooth
Strange tragedy of hypnotic
Loose words, loose teeth
Chew slowly lest you speak

In the devil's instant
We run from bake sale natter
Bus stop gossip
Neighborhood lament

Tell me a story
A life time
Save me
From
Words
Ill
Spent

The Urge to ask for life after we are dead

Streams of light
Former life
Energy never dies
Transformed they wait
Forlorn folk
Symptoms ranging;

Abused house wife
Pills and booze
Teenager lost in hormone dark
Jumped from bridge
Long time sufferer with yellow liver
Gas in car
Old and infirm
Rheumatism helped the fall
Custody battle father
His hunting gun

Their urge
So great
Spilling over
Enthusiasm
Just make it stop
This terrible
Unremitting pain
Of awareness

Find themselves
Suspended void
God or something entirely different
Absent
Feeling of weightlessness
No sense of light or dark
Stillness in airless abstract
Without earthly distraction

A question posed
Reflect
Do you want it back?
Now you have lost?
Pain
Both abhorred and familiar?
Back in time
Retrace just before

When it seemed there were no alternatives
Now
Would you do
It again?

Dissolving question
Choose
Return or stay
Until piece by piece
Memories of life
Fade
Joining stars and energy
Becoming
Nothing
Everything

What is your choice?

If we find ourselves here
An urge to ask for life
After we are dead
To empty listening post
Emptied earth souls
No going back
No staying still

Light
Be it divine or starlight fusion
Spilling through
Second chances
Forgotten
Remember
We exist, we cease
By hand, by fate
Once gone
No more
A
Choice
To
Make

Not even hemlock

Why do youth long to die
When life's so fond of them
So merciful, benign
Why do old seek death
Having lived such breadth
Surely a few more years left?
Yet as I wonder
Those who urge forward
Eternal sleep
In slowing of day
Witness
Dying light dissolve
Fading over valley

It is clear then
Our bond with death
As tangible as life
Infusing around us
Both parry and exist
Simultaneous
In echo and rebirth
One year to next
No wonder then
A stray impulse
To meet with life
Our end
And finally
Understand

Hurry

Hurry
We shall all be changed
By what happens
Now
Before awareness
And then
A time in cast, getting
Stronger like
Bones growing
Under skin

These beaten wings
Results of
Choices
Impossible to
Imagine before
Born on shore
They crawl to water

They are
Part of a long
Chain stretching
From our beginning
Where all is written
Saved for that purposed time
We fall into destined tread
Stepping over ancestors
Knowing and remaking
History with future
In hands that hold
All that has come before
And all that exists in
That hour we call
A lifetime

The short life

I never liked spiders, still don't
But your life
Viewed at distance
Impresses me
The size of your web
Effort taken to erect
Every rain storm
Next morning there you are again
Hours in dark
Perfect concentric circles in circles
Strong enough to make young branches
Bent toward you
In center
This one season
Like selling a house
Has to be completed by Fall
You too
Weathering 100 degree heat
Gather your cocooned children close
Watch over them
Until they hatch and bury in earth
That's when you die
I think too short a life
Though to you maybe
An eternity
One giant birth so many
Coming out of earth's sleep next year to take your place
And do it all again
I think I will be the only one sad
When I cannot see you in your web anymore
And wonder in my two dimensional human mind
At what moment you ceased
Where you went to dry back into soil
And of your bright color and determination
Somehow a sorrow that it is so fleeting
To me
A person who counts weeks as brief
I should see as you do
The value of life in minutes
And seconds
The fierce pulse
A strength
I fear
We've lost

The war of welts

Another conversation
Held in clenched fist
Silence
Disappointment
Ranging off window panes
Sliding behind sofa
With glasses off
Your face a blur
I don't want clarity
Instead
Watch
The welts
Of invisible
Insect bites
First redden
Itch
Sting
With white edges
Adding to older
That fade
My mottled arms
Well applied make up wasted
Drying on my face
Didn't I promise I'd never cry again?
Have this conversation again?
Be unable to act
Fear, cowardice, excuses, choose
From hat full
Guilt in that
Not taking the advice of enlightened souls
Too tired for self-help
Can't smoke can't drink
I'll wake with a rash
Bags underneath
Maybe want make up sex
Or to wring your neck
As you are
The snake around mine
Why stay and waste my time?
Why I cling in bouquet?
I can answer that
Love is madness
Lost in sadness
Full of passion

Intoxicated and
Invisible
Like bites
Reddening on my arms
I notice how old
This routine of ours
The dryness of wrists and elbows
I cannot bend in pose
A doll in flexible repose
My mind knows it knows
I'm smarter than this?
Others would say hell
With it
Cleverly I stay
An idiot in intelligent clothes
Stuffed with fury
Scratching bites
Wanting to smoke
Saying no
In control
Of nicotine
And
Wine
But not you
Not I

Absorbed paper cost

Some people don't like tapioca
Ya ya ya
We walk on stilts
Borrowing blankets of sky
Star parties
Underneath winking
Pitch
Humanities oil
This slippery consciousness
Leaking sincerity
In midnight flower
Killing bees, plucking life
Fitfully moon lights
What shined
In blink, ink, dark
Stretch of sky
Requiring
Infinity's
Fingerprint

Burst eardrums

They speak in tongues
Beneath my window
Mirrors catch their stares
Spooked by dragonflies
In listless drone
Please leave me out of this
Rough worn world
Let me close
My doors as flowers
Fold petals
Keep out
Of my solitary float
Dismantle your
Listening post
Take noise, take chore, take expectation, take knocking, ringing, endless demands for more
I have
Nothing
To give
It is late
Let us sleep
In hush
Bowed heads
Unspoken
Constant
Still
In empty
Hours
Slow
Turn

Old man's hunger

Extraordinary men
Are most often
Tempted
By
Ordinary
Things

He said
Rolling
Cigarette
Hanging
Languid
From
Thick fingers
Expensive shirt
Cuff links
Strong cologne

What would
You need
To be
Happy?

His children
And wife
In silver
Frame

Would this help?

His hands
Untying
Running
Like hot
Water
Pulling my
Naivety

I can give you
What you need

He pushes inside
No pretense of caring
All the way

Where it hurts
Hands pulling me
In cross stitch
His breath, expensive food
Whiskey
Money

You don't feel like
Anyone else

He thrusts deep
Starving
I hear my voice
I feel empty
Photo of his wife
Comforts me
Her face soft wax
A mother
Rounded stomach
He fills me
Spent on youth
Resting on jagged hip
Pinching my hollows

I love how thin you are
Your fragility, your cunt
Unstretched by birth

He eats my breast
Hurting me in differing ways
I see variation
is
His goal
To reverse age
Her gentle mothers
Curves
My breakable shallows
He is the child here
I know this
She knows this
He does not

Such is the arc of old man's
Fear
And
Hunger

Return me time

What I want
Is time

Forming in acrobatic
Brush stroke at
Urge of drum
Roll

The circus
Garish in transplant
Manipulated vault
On cusp of tight rope
Golden in repose

Return me time
On silver tray
Opening rose,
Closing day
Curtsey and fall

In incense sway
Priests in pirouette
Whirling dervish
Feet in unison
Rubbing floor clean
Sins bathed in
Receding shore

With you or without you
I only see you
I want time
Restored

To meet before
A lifeline
Claim years
We have not
In Memories vault

Choices
White skies
Burnt in
Chased

Blue and
Charcoal line
Silhouetted in
Journey from
Then
To
Now

Return to me

Time

Invert

Invert

Ask not
The mystery
Of an inverts
Heart

By nature
And ilk
She
Has no
Words
To share
Or spill

Ask not
The rhyme behind
Reticent eyes
Nor
The origin
Of shadows

Ask not
Why
Passing
Thought to pensive
Becomes
Mist
Penetrated only
In self

Ask not
To possess
Her light footed
Escape

It neither
Belongs to
You

Nor
This
World

Claimed instead
Wordless
Forest
A
Different
Pace

Where
Invert
Self may
Unfurl
Like fern

Finding solace
In
Deep earth
Rested silence
Red trees
Reaching
Higher
Into
Skies
Infinity

Inspired by Radclyffe Hall's *The Well Of Loneliness.*

Reflections advice

She told me
You get to a tipping point
Where everyone's younger

Invisible, as if handed a badge
Much like golden star
Or pink triangle
Stating
This woman's sell-by date expired
Do not consume

The irony of this, she said
Happens just as
You are in full bloom!

Longing to show off
Blunted edges of neurosis
It took two decades to tame
Longing to proclaim
I'm not your prisoner anymore!
Media, magazine, cellulite cream, bikini, tanning spray, under wire bra, lip gloss, hair
mousse, g- string, ribbed condom, raspberry lube, false eyelashes, Morning-After-Pill, love
letters, perennial hangover

She said, make mine a double
Let them laugh, it's a Blue Lagoon
I've drunk their Whiskey Sours, downed their Sex On The Beach and sniffed their proffered
powder

Time to be me
Age Of Sagittarius
Dawn of Not Giving A Shit
I'll go to bed with toys, in a long white nightdress, I won't floss, or avoid chocolate and
watch *Dynasty* on *Netflix*

With that she disappeared back
Into mirrored glass
Took a turn, checked her grays
Stroked age
With feathers
Loose fitting
Red gown
White wine and inimitable grace

Scorpion

You talk too well
And only convince me
To believe
What I know
Is untrue

As the scorpion
Stung
Saying only
It's my nature
To sting

Acts and intervals

I know something
About love
And loving

The short fused, wild hearted kind
Shining like polished stones underwater
And
A longer, enduring kind
Rising inexhaustibly
White smoke
Mountain top

Sometimes you want to hate feeling
Wretched play with parts of ourselves
Rarely articulated
Rolling glass
In our mouths
Until made smooth

Sit at table, sit in fever
Why don't you have some?
Eating fruit in sponge
Ethiopian coffee
With darkness
Reaching far outside
Like a rush of opera cloaks
Making for exit

Tabula-rasa

Ring a rosie
All fall down
Butcher, baker
Locust
Speak out loud

You were cold
I felt your neck for life
A moth's pulse
Flickering
In thin glass

You were dead
You came back to life
Doric in return
Lingua
Discrete history
Of moving silence

Racing nerves
Spiking
Rise out of this bed
Watch unscathed
Holding down
Three
Six arms

No forms here
Looking inside
Boxes within boxes
Tongues curled in fecund
Rendition
Growing old
Against long pause

Speak
Speak
Speak

Running out of air

I'm an indeterminate age
Somewhere between stations
Wherever you go
There you are

Waiting for Godot
No
The play never made sense

I was
A girl who walked in highlands
Hitching skirt over boots
Examining sheep's sculls
Bleached by wind to calcified chalk
Do they lay down
And die?
Just where we find them?
Can it really be
A series of rots and melts?
All they ever were
Into soil leaving rings of bodily
Fluid, like burnt wood
Left long marks the spot
Mushrooms grow out of
Soil enriched with former
Blood and fat, whatever else
Went into making her live
Yet
Nothing remains
Just wild, rolling hills
A small smooth skull
Cradled in chapped hands
To speak of being here
We so removed,
devolved from
harsh moors of ancestors
Tread
High mountain, thin air
Babies born by camp fire
The thrust and dying rape
Of modern notions
Forgotten here, with
a skull from unknown herd
Probably just over

Those hills
Where violet mist swirls
Shrouds
Things ahead of us
And where we came from
Keeping momentum
Steady and pure
Like high river water
And knowledge
We can neither run
From or to
Truth
It finds us
When we
Have
Run out
Of air

Granny the commie

Grandma
You relinquished your war crimes
Maintaining a semblance of dignity
Still not wearing a bra
Marx whispered in your ear
While supping down the local
With fags your husband hated
Oh how he loathed the queers
The only ones who
Sent flowers on your birthday
Knowing better than he
Your love of roses

Grandma
You should have been grandpa
Happier in trousers, elbows in soil
The honesty of tilling earth and toil
So far from gilded cage you dusted and mopped
A bride who wished she'd escaped the cake

This world was too young for your kind
Heart like a leaky bucket, kicking legs high,
Roll out the barrel! We'll have a barrel of fun!
Everyone came into your magic, pulling smiles like a magician
You'd sing; Never fear, I'll be here, drinking whiskey all the year
And doodle a cat on a serviette
Telling me
Go on lovey
Don't look back
Don't look back

For Freda

Damselfly

You
My Damselfly
Ethereal
Above
In warm air
Lightness catching
Setting sun
Tinsel and red
Shimmer reflection
Water a mirror
Of your
Everlasting
Impression
On
My
Heart

Kiss Kiss

I read today
on another mindless opinion site
Where people forget objectivity
And call rumor, fact
That
Men find among many things
Off-putting about women;
Sadness,
Negativity
and someone who reads too much

Whilst I'm only negative about certain enemies (murder, poverty, game-show hosts)
I do get sad
And I read frequently
The men who have pursued me must not mind
Or
A short skirt, great pair of legs and radiant humor
Makes up for it

However
The narrative of 3 off putting habits according to men…
Said
I didn't wear the skirt for you
I'm laughing at you
Not
With you
And this book I'm reading
Beat
Your
Witty repartee

Infasound

I hear
What you
Do not hear
Flatten my breasts
Shave my femininity
Into our lady of sorrow
Pluck my marrow in infasound
Find echo through divide
No more
Leave shoes at red door
Tuck cold toes
Bind in blanketing
Your thin legs, whirled like foxes chasing tails
released in surrendered fingertips
Foretold when touching my certain center, there came to be no separation
if you sing
Singed silver stars quilted in half circles
Her cheeks pinkening
As
We slowly form a
Whole
Moon

Acknowledgments

I work alone, but am inspired by many. Notably my thanks to; Crystal Kinistino, Johann Morton, Chuck Smith and Tim Arnold who always believed in my writing far more than I did.

To the artists I have read and been inspired by, to name but a few; Kate Bush, Radclyffe Hall, Patricia Highsmith, The Bronte sisters, Adrienne Rich, Gwendolyn Brooks, *Ballet Rambert Dance Company*, Octavio Paz, Gerard Manley Hopkins, E.E., Cummings, Gabriel Garcia Marquez, Roald Dahl, Shel Silverstein, Peter Gabriel, Jean Cocteau, Pink Floyd, Pablo Neruda, Anne Sexton, Maya Angelou, Toni Morrison, Arnold Lobel, Joan Aiken, Angela Carter, Maurice Sendak, C.S., Lewis, Elizabeth Smart and countless children's authors and illustrators.

To all the lovely people I have met on *WordPress* via my site *TheFeatheredSleep*, without whom I should not have encouragement to keep writing. Thank you so much for your words.